Other titles in the UWAP Poetry series (established 2016)

Our Lady of the Fence Post by J. H. Crone

Border Security by Bruce Dawe

Melbourne Journal by Alan Loney

Star Struck by David McCooey

Dark Convicts by Judy Johnson

Rallying by Quinn Eades

Flute of Milk by Susan Fealy

A Personal History of Vision by Luke Fischer

Snake Like Charms by Amanda Joy

Charlie Twirl by Alan Gould

Afloat in Light by David Adès

Communists Like Us by John Falzon

Preparations for Departure by Nathanael O'Reilly

Praise for Previous Work

Conversational, intelligent, wide-ranging and witty, Hecq's poetry is distinguished, too, by its acerbic tone and its confidence—LISA GORTON

... roaming in her poetry between experimentation and high tradition... Hecq targets the self-reflexive play of language—ANTHONY LYNCH

This is erudite writing with a reflexive impulse. With flashes of humour—in even its darkest material. Writing with a restless heart—NOËLLE JANANCZEWSKA

... Hecq displays her predominant interest in celebrating poetry and word to relate the life that is given to the reader—VIVIENNE PLUMB

... Hecq's writing shows us that the power of language lies less in what words can say than in what worlds of experience their music can evoke—HELEN GILFIND

A work of high originality and courage, which composes a new music, compelling and uncanny, by sounding the often untranslatable abyss between beings and sexes—MARION MAY CAMPBELL

... readers will come away feeling renewed, invigorated, deeply inspired by Hecq's unique talent—RICHARD HILLMAN

The uncanny pleasures of this text are many—the precision of the language, the weaving of myth into the everyday, the distinctiveness of the narrative voice, the poetic conjunction of events—FIONA CAPP

Out of Bounds probes the rhetoric of chance invoked as a symbolic structure. Violent, active, disturbing—MICHAEL FARRELL

A fascinating and deeply engrossing philosophical fable... In *Out of Bounds* Hecq has created a superb personal scripture—ALI ALIZADEH

In *Couchgrass*, Dominique Hecq breaks through the surfaces of the everyday to reach the garden of tangled connections in which we find our life roots—MARIA TAKOLANDER

Like poetry itself, couchgrass spreads everywhere despite one's best efforts to eradicate it. Invasive, rhizomic, a denizen of cracks and crannies, couchgrass also has antibiotic properties. Like couchgrass, Dominique Hecq's latest book will establish its little fibrous roots even in the mind's most unpropitious earth—JUSTIN CLEMENS

Books by Dominique Hecq

(2017) with Julian Novitz, eds. *Creative Writing with Critical Theory: Inhabitation*. Canterbury: Gylphi.

(2015) *Towards a Poetics of Creative Writing*. Bristol; Buffalo; Toronto: Multilingual Matters.

(2015) with Russell Grigg and Craig Smith, eds. *Female Sexuality: The Early Psychoanalytic Controversies*. London: Karnac Books. (Republished)

(2014) *Stretchmarks of Sun*. Melbourne: Re.Press. [Poetry]

(2012) *The Creativity Market: Creative Writing in the 21st Century*. Bristol; Buffalo; Toronto: Multilingual Matters.

(2009) *Out of Bounds*. Prahran, Vic: Re.Press. [Poetry]

(2006) *Couchgrass*. Linton, Vic: Papyrus Publishing. [Poetry]

(2004) *Noisy Blood: Stories*. Scarsdale, Vic: Papyrus Publishing. [Short Stories]

(2002) *Good Grief: and Other Frivolous Journeys into Spells, Songs and Elegies*. Scarsdale, Vic: Papyrus Publishing. [Poetry]

(2000) *The Book of Elsa*. Upper Ferntree Gully, Vic: Papyrus Publishing. [Novel]

(2000) *Magic and Other Stories*. Macclesfield, Vic: Woorilla. [Short Stories]

(1999) with Russell Grigg and Craig Smith *Female Sexuality: The Early Psychoanalytic Controversies*. London: Rebus Press.

(1999) *The Gaze of Silence*. Enfield Plaza, South Australia: Sidewalk Collective. [Poetry]

(1999) *Mythfits: Four Uneasy Pieces*. Blackburn, Vic: PenFolk Publishing. [Short Stories]

Dominique Hecq

Dominique Hecq grew up in the French-speaking part of Belgium. She read Germanic Philology at the University of Liège and then flew over to Australia where she completed a PhD on exile in Australian Literature. She also holds an MA in Literary Translation. Dominique is the author of a novel, three collections of short fiction, five books of poetry and two plays. Her awards include The New England Review Prize for Poetry (2005), The Martha Richardson Medal for Poetry (2006), and the inaugural AALITRA Prize for Literary Translation in poetry from Spanish into English (2014). *Hush: a fugue* (2017) is her latest book of poetry.

Dominique Hecq
Hush
a fugue

First published in 2017 by
UWA Publishing
Crawley, Western Australia 6009
www.uwap.uwa.edu.au

UWAP is an imprint of UWA Publishing
a division of The University of Western Australia

This book is copyright. Apart from any fair dealing
for the purpose of private study, research, criticism
or review, as permitted under the *Copyright Act 1968*,
no part may be reproduced by any process without
written permission.
Enquiries should be made to the publisher.

Copyright © Dominique Hecq 2017
The moral right of the author has been asserted.

National Library of Australia
Cataloguing-in-Publication entry:
Hecq, Dominique, author.
Hush : a fugue / Dominique Hecq.
ISBN: 9781742589473 (paperback)
Includes bibliographical references.
Poetry—Collections.
Australian poetry—21st century.

Designed by Becky Chilcott, Chil3
Typeset in Lyon Text by Lasertype
Printed by McPherson's Printing Group

 uwapublishing

for David

The spirit-child is an unwilling adventurer into chaos and sunlight, into the dreams of the living child

Ben Okri

Acknowledgements

Some of the pieces in this book were published elsewhere, bearing a title that has been removed here for the purposes of aesthetic integrity. Grateful acknowledgements are due to the editors of the following publications:

1110: One Photograph One Story Ten Poems 2: "Oranges and Lemons"

Double Dialogues: In/Stead 3: "Alabaster"

Double Dialogues 17: "Reading in Braille"

Centoria 4: "Strawberries"

Food and Appetites: The Hunger Artist and the Arts (Cambridge Scholars Publishing, 2012): "Blue Like an Orange"

Good Grief (Papyrus Publishing, 2002): "Strawberries"

La Traductière 30: "Reading in Braille"

Meniscus 1:1: "Tomorrow, the Sun"

Meniscus 2:2: "Felt"

Offshoot (University of Western Australia Publishing, 2017): "Quickening"

TEXT: Journal of Writing and Writing Courses Special Issue 7: "Glitter"

TEXT Journal of Writing and Writing Courses 15:2: "Oranges and Lemons"

TEXT Journal of Writing and Writing Courses Special Issue 35: "Crypts of Making"

The Invention of Legacy (Rodopi, 2016): "Letters to the End of Grief"

Towards a Poetics of Creative Writing (Multilingual Matters 2015): "Blue Like an Orange"

Profound thanks to Sari Smith, Elizabeth Colbert, Christine Hill, Julia Prendergast and Stephen Theiler, who kept me going in the darkest times. For their generosity, thanks to Katharine Coles and Dan Disney. Thanks to Luke, Paul, Jerome, Emmanuel and Xavier Murphy. And, finally, thanks to Terri-ann White and her fabulous team at UWA Publishing.

Led astray by a smattering of wild strawberries one early morning in June, I wandered off into the neighbour's garden. I was not aware of doing anything odd: a scent of roses, carnations and a late-blooming lilac, the sheer beauty of the lime tree showering pollen. I was startled by my grandmother's troubled and insistent voice calling out for me. Calling out. Calling.

It is some thirty years after my grandmother's troubled search for me that I recalled, on the loss of my second son, that quiet dawn in the garden all the way back in the northern hemisphere.

> *Eurydice, Eurydice, Eurydice.*

Three times Orpheus called in vain. That passage in the Underworld haunts me. So did the many paintings and stories of children lost in the Bush when I first came to Australia, especially the tragic tale of three young boys who wandered off at dusk into the chill of one June day one hundred and fifty years ago, never to return.

> The little girl at dawn
> in her night gown
> sun smattered
> strawberries in her hands
> opens the world and sweet
> ripe words spill
>
> Where is she?

My grandmother had a secret reason to be worried about losing me. I now recall finding myself staring at the photo of baby Zeno, her second child, weirdly dressed in his cot. A white cloth binds his head. He is wearing a long white dress; pinned on it, a Sacred Heart badge. The photo is black and white and so I can only imagine the colours. The heart is red and bleeding.

I must have wondered why baby Zeno looked so much like a porcelain doll. I must have asked why.

> Shh, shh, shh, Zeno is in heaven, said my grandmother with a mixture of sadness and shock in her voice. You must say a prayer for him, and apologise to God for calling him baby Zero.

In the year 1994 I lost a brother and a child, one to a freak accident, the other to ill-health. All lies. But how to speak of suicide and cot-death in a family where life is meant to be a gift? My grandmother did not survive these lies. She lost the will to live after my brother's death. The news of my baby's sudden death most certainly hastened her own. Like me, she stopped eating. Like me, she stopped speaking.

> The little girl at dawn
> in her night gown
> sun smattered
> strawberries in her hands
> opens the world and sweet
> ripe words spill

The truth is in between. It is the story stripped of guilt and fear, for neither fear nor guilt feed the imagination needed to go on living.

What are we made of but longing and sorrow, love and loss? Bruised strawberries in the morning sun.

Grief becomes an echo of echoes, a chancy affair for which we can't be prepared. In this echoing, the voice of Orpheus calls:

> *Eurydice, Eurydice, Eurydice.*

Morning hail

    gusts of wind

        moaning

Halfway through 1994, I believed the worst of the year was over. We lived in a rented house in the inner suburbs of Melbourne. It was a changeable house. Sometimes it felt safe as a church, and sometimes it shivered and cracked apart. A sloping slate roof held it down, pressing heat on us in summer, blowing cold in winter. What kept the house together was skin. Walls of cream gristle called *crépi*.

It was June 30th, an ordinary crisp winter day. Sunshine and magpies everywhere. After lunch, I took the children for a walk. His hands barely reaching the pram's handle, my first-born insisted on pushing his baby brother. Along the Merri Creek, there were egrets and ibises and ducks. Some turtles and tiny frogs. We sang duck songs and frog songs. I made up a magpie story as we passed a whole family of them. We bought quinces on the way back and I baked an upside-down quince cake. I was almost getting serious about planting winter vegetables, cornflowers and the last bulbs of irises, jonquils and ranunculi before nightfall when I decided against it.

Nights close early in June. Everything seems to stand still, bleak, even gloomy by five. I bundled the children inside the house, drew the curtains and flicked on the lights. It felt safe despite the cold air curling at our feet.

When I turned off the lights well after bed-time, I looked through the window. The roses looked dead but for a few white buds on their maimed limbs.

>Why is white white?
>
>Chalk, rice, zinc
>>Crystal falls
>>>Limestone graves
>
>Phosphorus
>>Lightless body
>>>Alabaster

I woke up in the night, chilled as the whites in a Dutch still-life painting.

    A still-life belongs to time, and we to this stillness.

    In his cot, my baby's face was white wax
                            as if smothered by the moon itself.

    His lips were black.

    My voice died out in my scream.

    My voice died out in my scream.

    Life goes on, they say. Life goes on leaving
    me—a hiatus.

    I became the copula between life and death.

    An object with no voice.

    Mère echo ooooooooo

    Why is white white?

    Chalk, rice, zinc
            Crystal falls
                Limestone graves

    Phosphorus
            Lightless body
                Alabaster

Mère echo oooooooooo

Why is white white?

    An orchestra
        in a guitar
            colour cascades

                i
              n
             w
              h
               y
              t
                e

             W
H
                       Y
          t
       e

               W
                   H
           Y
                  t

              e

            W
       H
                          Y
         te — eeeeeee

Literature is like phosphorus, Barthes says in *Writing Degree Zero*.

It shines with its maximum brilliance at the moment when it attempts to die.

For Barthes, literature is always already a posthumous affair.

And so he tricked himself to write out the white into brilliance.

White paint comes from many things—chalk, rice, zinc, quartz, alabaster, lead.

Vermeer made some of his luminescent whites from alabaster and quartz—in lumps that took the light into the painting and made it wriggle and dance.

    White is white because it reflects light off.

The price white pays for this sheer purity is that it absorbs no light into its own body—and for lead white, this means its own heart is black.

And so I tricked myself to write the white into glitter from the black of my heart.

    Chalk, rice, zinc
        crystal falls
            Limestone graves

    Phosphorus
        Lightless body
            Alabaster

From my limestone grave, a foreign voice came out.

In-crypted, I wrote myself out into a make-believe.

For the impossibility of saying nothing. Of not saying anything. Of not saying. Of saying.

For the sheer possibility of putting death to death.

The priest's words

        rise into the air

The ground drops

        under my feet

After the funeral I looked for sustenance in the sky. But the light was out to blind me. It fell through the branches of gum trees like numb fingers thumbing through clouds for words to name the wind. All it found were synonyms for blue as though nothing comforts the eye but light and shade pacing through hues and meanings of blue.

Lapis-lazuli azure cobalt and navy and sapphire and cerulean. Tearful blue, sad, low, despondent, dejected, melancholy, desolate. But most of all lapis-lazuli with veins yielding azure indigo and ultramarine. Azure light enough to allow the sun to flood through. Cobalt, harsh and sharp. Indigo. And ultramarine that tastes of the sea, salty, smooth and warm. Ultra deep depth. The veined mingling of violet and green shooting through purple that is close to red: green that is close to yellow and yellow that is close to orange.

What I saw in the sky when the rays of the sun lay flat upon my hand was a black sea I dipped into. And ducked out of.

The Mother, for lack of a proper name, formerly myself, listened for the click of the latch in the frame of the front door. She listened for the voice that would ask her a question. She listened and heard a voice.

> The wind. The wind yowling.
>
> No words.
>
> What are words for? You ask.

She felt as though she had forgotten what it was like to lift her tongue, what it was like to lick her lips unstuck, what it was like to outlive the cold. To live.

It all seemed to have blown away from her. Out of reach of her body. Her memory, cut loose. This, she thought, is what it feels like to be dead.

Dead.

The word entered the Mother's head. It took up residence there and multiplied.

How a word can kill.

My feet pushed her away and across the room, across the passage and into the corridor. Out onto the verandah. Carried her back into a time before that now time. She sniffed the air and fell in a cloud of musty dust. Vanished in the sky.

She could have screamed, but willed her eyes open. It just couldn't be true. The mother was going to wake up to the call of her baby, tune her ear to the sound of people talking in the street, the muffled roar of motorcars passing her window, the clamour of schoolchildren hurrying to school, all in one clap out of this room and into the cold of a brand new morning.

Today—yes, she thought, she will bake a cake, a lemon and almond cake, with lemons and almonds from her trees to celebrate the promise of the brand new day. Today—yes! She will be frivolous. She will dress up and dress the children in matching clothes the way they do in children's books and women's magazines. She will go to the market and buy flowers and food. They will listen to market music from the Andes. She will buy bunches of tulips, irises and jonquils as bright and lush as she can find. And she will buy oranges and chestnuts, cherry tomatoes and golden spuds, swedes and parsnips, a tiny pumpkin. Asparagus, perhaps. Tarragon and thyme, garlic and ginger. And today—yes! She will surprise them all. Her family.

He will come home at six and he will say hmm whatever it is it smells fantastic and he will ask what did our little king do today? And he will kiss the first-born and the Mother and perhaps listen to the answer and then he will open his violin case and play something, something soft and crisp by Paganini and the new baby will look at his father and give him his first smile so that he too can delight as the Mother did in something as fleeting and precious as that. Then they will eat.

What I saw in the sky when the rays of the sun lay flat upon my hand was a black sea I dipped into. And ducked out of: it was cold.

I ducked out of the black sea of blue for in this life meant to be starting all over again there was an endless series of things to be done, meals to be cooked. All in an endless time of grief not to be done. On hold. Grief in ashes for life's sake. For the first-born's sake, the sleeping boy who now refused to speak his mother tongue, the one to whom I'd said I have you and we'll get through this.

When the night fell on the day of the funeral and our voices hushed and in the immense sweetness of the blue night all I heard was the child, the first one, breathing.

It was a matter of existing between the deep centre and the vast periphery. But time would not flow. Time was hard honey. Amber. Ambergris. *Gris* not blue. Blue-grey.

I was a time bomb waiting to explode. Longed for food. Warmth. I felt so cold. At night my want was so strong I stared at the corner between the ceiling and wall, and a single, giant eye would appear. I could not or would not move that gigantic eye. I could not make it blink. Make it disappear. My body lay cold and rigid and empty. Apart from me. I was hollow, and in the hole was that eye, endlessly staring.

I stared into the void in my life. Into the hole in my heart. I devoured books on cot death, filled my ears with interviews of professionals and parents who had been touched by it. I read to the child and helped him draw his own story of loss in a ledger adorned with stars. I cooked.

There were pancakes and French toast and brioche. Lemon pudding and orange cake and rhubarb pie and apple crumble. Poppy seed cake. Marzipan. Blueberry muffins. Roasted chestnuts and peppers and eggplants we called aubergines still. Artichoke hearts were preserved, for the child liked the leaves. There were cats' tongues and profiteroles and jalousies. Gingerbread men and gingerbread stars.

I longed for food, in whatever form. I felt so greedy, and yet it cut me off from the child and from his father too. I would not eat. There was no room for me. I rose and fell. Rose and fell. Flailed around me in a sea of black. Lack. Living and wanting to die. I fell into the waterfall of my mind. I had been there before.

Eating and I. Smoking and I. These had been the staples of my life. I had made them my life. One after the other. One the other side of the other. I had blown them up into huge bunches of flowers: irises and daffodils spiked alternately, gerberas arranged in incremental hues of lemon, orange, crimson, scarlet, sienna. Cambridge bells, bluebells, cornflowers, periwinkle and gypsophile. Hollyhocks. Red roses. *Petals of blood.* Asphodels and lilies and jonquils and hyacinths.

Now that part of me had died for real, it felt more difficult to sort out the irises from the hyacinths, the daffodils from the jonquils. Spellbound and sickened by the smells, I almost forgot life in the process.

The fear of eating was huge. Palpable. Time would not flow. Time was rock hard. Amber. I was cold and empty. I could not eat lest I implode with guilt or explode with anger. All meaning disintegrated and hit me hard where my heart should have been.

The fear of smoking was thin, like a mist that would surface in dreams.

Loving that disposal of greed. Loving that being painted into a corner, you see.

I listenened to music. Thought it would fill the hole. I listened to Kinchela's 'Mourned by the wind' and nearly cried. It was a solace as tangible as if some other sentient being had been affirming my own sorrow. But I could not listen. Would not take any risks. No, not then. I asked myself what if I entered down into the numb emptiness of my life. But saw I couldn't go there, for the sake of the child. I sensed there was another dimension there. Movement. Slow. Space. Sparse. And absolute nothingness.

Hunger was the obvious answer, like an atheist's prayer.

I tried writing. Words came in bursts and spurts. Made no sense.

I had lost my alphabet in the night sky.

> What did I want?
> Misprint.
> A copyist's error.
> Never before had I asked myself that question.

I was a ghost on a ghost train. Had been on it for so long. It was the story of my life. I knew the terror. Knew the uncanny creatures and their accoutrements: those that spring out at you, cackling. Always the same place, same time. Here.

Gossamer, the scent of jonquils and hyacinths.

> Diaphanous bodies
>   ghosts that will kick you in the shins
>   knife you in the back
> dead stars dancing before your eyes
>   strings of pearls
>   showers of confetti
>   fog steaming up.

The old woman pushing her cart, not even hiding her scythe.

And the fear, always the fear.

I would not cry. The wind blew through the house like in a book
I read as a child about a girl who was lost. The wind. Perhaps,
I thought, it would crack the lemon tree, the one whose lemons
I make lemonade with. The one where ghosts rest and whisper, the
one the wind would crack. Expose the back of the leaves, polish their
dust off. All you could hear was the wind.

> Words lost.

> Voice gone.

> All had broken with the voice of the dead.

> How dare the phone ring.

Consistency, routine, the structures you get used to, make us
believe all lies as truth; lies throttled by a telephone cord in the late
afternoon.

The fear was so strong I bolted for the door and into the street. I ran
to the park as fast as thoughts ran through my mind. I ran oblivious to
the traffic. Oblivious to time. Oblivious of the cold. I ran to the pond.
And stood. When the shadows merged with the waters in the cold,
when the wind moaned in the branches of the gum trees, when the
last rays of sunshine gilded with mystery the white snowdrops and
camellias, I turned back home.

I did not know what my thoughts were, what kind of feelings were
coursing through my veins, nor did I know why I had to go through
this. All I knew then was that I needed to write for the sheer
satisfaction of keeping fear at bay, of experiencing the vanity of
meaning, even if words did not make sense.

Blue like an orange.

The dark is stitched with points of light and all the threads at the back of the sky make the lining of the universe.

It is odd, this urge to write out of fear. Out of the fear of succumbing to sorrow. A sorrow with far more distant echoes than this mewling of the wind.

    Why do we think and speak?

This is a child's question, just like, why is the sky blue? You should be able to answer it, but can only offer a reprint: *blue like an orange.*

This is a lie. It is the earth which is blue like an orange. For you can eat oranges as we do the earth. For alongside the hunger for food is a deeper hunger that is thwarted.

That's why you lie. Use metaphors. Fast and write.

And you need to check your thoughts for we christened the stars without thinking they needed no names and the numbers that are comets do cross the dark and land on virgin vines like chains of red pepper that crawl in the wind that whistles soft and sad as a flute in the twilight.

As I wrote, compelled back to the black sea, I felt my heart expanding towards the sky and tears came to my eyes for the first time since death had been.

It is odd our tears, shed or unshed, do not speak, and yet we seem to understand them and the sound of a child scuttling through the front door is sweeter than words.

    Mummy, I'm hungry.

Dark then light

    Uno makes rainbows

        doubling the sky

The neighbour says babies are like clocks. Sometimes they stop ticking. Tick. Tock. Tick.

Her black cat is at our back door meowing for food. I feel mean, but shoo him away. Kick. Kick.

When I come back into the kitchen the child has gone. I can hear him talking to someone. I find him in the front passage, perched on a stool next to the telephone. He hands me the receiver:
    My lady wants to talk to you.
Apparently, he's been calling this random number for some time without his mostly absent and aphasic mother noticing. I apologise.

Now the child has my pink swim cap on. His eyes are hidden behind his father's scratched goggles. This is his rock-'n'-roll outfit. A slow strum comes out of the guitar. Another one, followed by rapid drumming.

The child looks up, beaming. Strum. Drum. Strum. Drum... Drum. Drum.

> Mummy.
> Yes, love.
> You know father Victor.
> Mm.
> He has baby Jesus around his neck.
> That's right. It's called a crucifix.
> Why did he turn the cross around on his chest the other day?
> Because he doesn't want god to see he loves his food.

> Strum. Drum. Strum. Drum... Drum. Drum. Drum.

> *Muum.* Was your brother *bloodied* when he *die-ded*?
> No. He looked exactly like in the photo on my desk.
> But why did he kill *hisself*?
> Ah, that's another story.

The child is waiting for the full reply. He takes off his goggles. Peels off his swim cap. Looks at me. Expectantly.

I don't quite know where to begin.

Where to end.

I suggest a walk to the park with the water spouting from the ground for inspiration. But not before we have left a Tim Tam for his mouse.

>High five! The child slips his hand into mine.

Jacaranda blooms

bursting through

For a while it seemed we had been mad about the sky. And then the sky became our calendar.

Moon, sun, stars, like so many signs to guide us through time.

The world crumpling like a dying supernova.

One morning before dawn, I stood on a cliff-top above Beehive Falls in the Grampians. Ecstatic. In despair. I spread my arms and uttered a primal cry.

The waterfall kept running.

The darkness before dawn remained dark.

>   Chalk, rice, zinc
>   Crystal falls
>   Limestone graves
>
>   Phosphorus
>   Lightless body
>   Alabaster

And then, that glorious sunlight.

In the darkness, there came a turning. It was as though the dark itself offered a *leitmotif*. At that point I saw just two qualities: an ability to *be*, and to be *attentive*. Contemplating that tight space, I was aware of some presence, aware of spirits inhabiting the apparent void, aware of the long and newly dead. There, in that *inbetween* space, everything seemed to come together. In the light of this inward sun, it all made sense again.

The turning happened. I surrendered to some invisible force. An inner world opened up in me. I began to walk and as I walked I began to speak again. Wotwuwhoosh whoosh whooshwooo... moon, sun, stars... whoosh... wooo...

My legs walked me to the grey house, the one our hosts call the cabin. The ground crackled under my feet. It was hard to think. On the footpath, a dead bird. I started skipping. Meantime, I cried to the skies. Moon. Sun. Stars. Meanwhile, somewhere life had just begun.

When I pushed open the door of the cabin, father and son, wrapped in patchwork doona, were reading *The Giant Book of Trucks*.

I would have to cook breakfast. The man would want bacon and eggs. The child would want pancakes. We would need steaming hot coffee and hot chocolate. *Tra la lalala*. I have lost my place in the world. *Tra la lalala*.

I foxed my way through the living room and down a dim corridor of deepening greys.

In the master bedroom's half-light, the threefold mirror shows off its dusty face across two cracks. In the faint light I turn away from liquid ash as a child turns in vain around her own reflection. Plonk myself down on the bed, adjust the pillow behind my back, pick up the notebook and the pencil from the bedside table and scribble.

> *~~(M)otherwise~~*
> *~~Womb with a view (navel gazing)~~—nothing to do with it*
> *~~Tomb with a view~~ (too specific to account for ~~narrative~~ artistic impulse)*
> *The blind leading the blind, as usual and I must remember to ditch that overcooked book.*
>
>
> *Reading in Braille*
>
> *Against the heavy sky*
> *day after day you live*
> *and look for words*
> *under your own eyelids.*

*In the darkness comes a turning
where everything leads to this
inbetween
this inward sun.*

*And so you write
the way you hang
the washing out
pegs in your mouth
knowing full well
it's not Monday.*

*The sun dictates our daily tasks
and the prayers that rise
towards the newly dead
like butterflies
surrendering to every breath.*

Hmm. Butterflies surrendering to every breath of air sounds like a European conceit. Like pink flower petals. White roses. Our roses are black. Like stars becoming black holes. *Tra la lalala...*

My star, a black hole: the one whose gravity prevents any light from escaping.

And now breakfast: pancakes for everyone. But one.

Here I go back to my place, in a cloud of smoke.

Only to realise things have shifted.

The father has made coffee and is busy with his Sudoku.

The child is drawing in charcoal on the walls of the cabin. He draws a lion under a canopy of stars which look all the more dramatic because of the yellow all over the walls that create a swirling caramel effect.

I take a mixing bowl from the drying rack and place it on the bench next to the pantry cupboard. My hands open the cupboard as I think of ink. The right hand reaches for the flour container and as it does I get a whiff of vanilla and cloves. The hand finds the cup and the cup ploughs in the flour, scoops it up and dips it in the bowl. Hands make a well. Find eggs and milk in the fridge. Break three eggs, pour two cups of milk. Stir. Whisk. Add a tablespoon of oil. Meanwhile, I think of ink.

In the Renaissance it was desirable to have ink that not only travelled seductively across the paper, but which also smelled wonderful. To make writing the sensual experience scholars desired they experimented with vanilla, cloves, honey, locusts, the virgin pressing of olives, powdered mother of pearl, scented musk, rhinoceros horn, jade, jasper, pine, wine...

Almost forgot the secret ingredient: water. Oil in the pan. Heat. Swirl it around so it won't stick. Now. Shprshhhhhh!

Hebborn's recipe for ink is versatile; the result a variety of hues from deep yellow to black. Mix water or wine with gum Arabic, galls and coconut kernels and leave the stew covered under warm sunlight for several days. Rotten acorns as good as gall. As for the wine, he preferred to drink it rather than add it to the brew.

First pancake black. Turn down the heat.

Our days are bracketed now, or so it seems to me.

The father shot a rabbit last night and skinned it. I cooked it with prunes. The child spared the bones and tomorrow he will patiently put them together again.

As I finished the washing up and the man read to the child after dinner the sun had set, bringing the sky low and spreading thin clouds into the corners of the horizon where the light was still standing. It was getting dark now. The sun had dipped below the side of the mountain and I imagined the sky in the West was draining quickly into the Beehive Falls inset. I felt compelled to return.

It was a cloudless night and the moon was surfacing above the top of the hill, casting before it a net of brightness that crept up and up and made new shadows in the ground. Half-way up the hill I stopped in the cover of a twisted she-oak that was leaning over the path, the smell of tea-tree, eucalypt and humus straining my nostrils. And there he was: the angel stood in the middle of the path, swaying on his feet as he looked straight ahead, oblivious to the world of the living. I stood still. He shifted from one foot to the other, then set off into the shadows. I hung back. Above me lay the iridescent outline of the hill, barely lit by the sinking sun.

We are back where we call it home, our cream *crépi* house in Melbourne and as both father and child sleep, it suddenly hits me. Here is my desk. Here is where I have existed for so many years. Here is the crude palimpsest of my being since setting foot in this country. I open the top drawer. Instead of encountering the familiar soft-rough feel of manila folders, my fingers meet the cold of a plastic pouch. The pouch, I see and now also recall, contains a pale yellow matinee jacket and matching bootees knitted in angora wool I salvaged from the charity bag when our baby's clothes and toys were being packed away. The wool is soft and unctuous. It smells of caramel.

Tomorrow is Tuesday. Garbage day. I have some work to do.

I sit in jubilation as I watch the garbos pack up and trash the box labelled 'Last draft and floppy disks for *Exile Down Under*.' Inexplicably, I find poise and presence and being. Then there is the momentarily arrested gasp of surprise.

The child, I forget to say, is with me. And he laughs with me, too, as the box disappears in the crushing backside of the truck.

Viridian wiggles

    on the fence

        chuckle lips unstuck

At night time I heard steps rushing through the corridor. A cold draught fell on me. The door opened by itself and a crowd of people entered our bedroom, perhaps six or seven—I barely had time to count them. They were tall and small, fat and thin. They had blank faces, yellow eyes and lips the colour of blackcurrants. I blinked. They drew back the curtains at my window, each pointing to the fawn moon with their long middle finger. They gazed at me from their large lidless yellow eyes. I stared back, lost for words. They laughed, their laughter a rattle. And they left.

It was, I first thought, the yellow eyes that drove me away. Now I know it was fear tinged with guilt, and hope, too.

As I left the room I glanced at the night-tousled hair on the pillow next to mine: he often sleeps face down, like an overgrown baby. I rushed to the front passage, picked up my keys from their hook, went back for my woollen scarf, locked the door and pressed into the shadows.

October, the middle of spring, the time when gardens seem to grow overnight. I could smell the lilac as the wind pounded my back on my way to the car. I got in and sank into myself, or the idea of myself. In an hour's time I would be sweeping through a sea of blackwoods in bloom. In an hour's time I would be catching up with the source of this unusually icy wind. In an hour's time I would be boarding a plane into some rainbow, or the recollection of some rainbow.

And tomorrow...

Well, tomorrow would be light shining on a leaf, a daub of paint, a knob of butter.

I headed for the highway, reluctantly breathing in the chilled sulphurous smells of factories, unnerved by the lingering yellow light in the night sky. Yellow, a colour I now loathed, perhaps because I had become aware of its ambiguous connotations: the colour of pulsating

life—of corn and sunshine and gold and angelic haloes, but also...
Let's not get into that.

Ours wasn't such a bad marriage. But it always felt as if someone had stolen my paintbox, leaving behind grey harmonies. While I longed for stark, pencil-drawn pictures, harmonies always turned messy, absorbing the lighter shades, obliterating the black traits. And so, instead of wiping clean the smudge under the guttering of the suburbs, I dabbed at it again and again.

He was looking over my shoulder when I ran my sable brush swiftly across the canvas of *Waves Breaking at Sandy Point*. It carried a ruby slick of oil paint where the sun's last colours were supposed to hit the clouds. But when I looked at what I'd done, the carmine pigment, like the day I had been imagining, together with its palpable paradoxes, had vanished. Instead, the painting showed a grey wash over a dull afternoon.

> I don't know that you really care, I said.
> Do you?
> I said to you the other day—I said, now that the ... the ... the baby is no longer with us there doesn't seem to be any point to it— And do you recall what you answered?
> Not exactly.
> You said, It never seemed there was much point anyway. And do you know what I thought?
> No, though it's not hard to guess.
> Well, I thought, and to think I married you for this. What a fucking waste.
> I hated to hear the person I had become: mean, brittle, volatile, vindictive.
> Shh. Shh. Shh, you said, exciting my rage.

It was hard not to feel enraged again. I tried focusing on the road. I turned the radio on. Turned it off. Music was painful to hear.

Submerged in lines of rain shattering all around me it was above all painful to remember loss—Eurydice, Eurydice, Eurydice.

I knew no melody to coax my fury, no rhythm to say time knows nothing about abjection, no words to tame guilt, and no silence or *da capo* to convey this—yes, *this revolting sliver of hope*.

I pushed on, whooshing through wet deserted streets, imagining myself airborne. As I reached the highway I eased the car into the right-hand lane and stopped at the green light.

It's not easy being green, I sang, emulating the frog puppet from *Sesame Street*.

A taxi tooted, shocking me into consciousness and movement. The car picked up speed. Scandalously, the green frog morphed into the Chinese poet Xu Yin who once wrote about *mi se*, the mysterious greenish hue.

Carving the light from the moon to dye the mountain stream.

Away! I was suddenly transported far away from everywhere and everything. I was nowhere. I could suddenly go back to where home was, or not. It didn't matter. I was empty, absent, too full. Nowhere. I was gone.

I was going to write the story of *mi se*.

Then I saw blue flashes. They got thicker and thicker. I couldn't see things any longer. Couldn't see past my luminous windscreen. Couldn't see the road for the flashes. I panicked. I didn't want to be noticed. I stopped the car. Everything was blue. I shut my eyes and held on as long as I could. I hurt everywhere. I heard a car door slam. I heard voices. As my own voice boomed out of my body something burst and it was all over. I was empty again. I opened my eyes. The light inside my car was on. The window on the driver's side was wound down. Rain was falling slant on the dashboard. Beads of water were scattered on my jumper. My face and hands were damp. Outside, the night was pouring in thick sheets. I folded my speeding ticket, shoved it in the glove-box, and drove off.

It is strange how pain comes and goes. The pain had definitely gone. There was just a dull ache. With this realisation I was tempted to turn around as if my life, too, could be turned around. But wisdom has it that there are no escape routes. There are no real U-turns either. Perhaps destiny is but a series of cross-roads and dead ends.

I kept driving.

It was getting colder and apart from the odd emergency phone booth on the side of the highway, the landscape was now a sea of grey mist. I longed for the winding country road, its lonesome tree silhouettes, the spectral properties outlined haphazardly in the dark, the narrow bridge out of the forest, the climb up the hill. Soon.

I turned the radio on, changed band to AM and tuned into a drama show. A new play titled *The Amazon* was being discussed. Coming from an upper-middle-class family, the Amazon scares both men and women as soon as she appears in a psychodrama group: six foot, an Audi TT, the ease of a model, the voice of a man, with a frankly scabrous language; women stop speaking and men look down. The Amazon is divorced. She now feels great remorse for this as she has not been able to keep her child. This loss is irreparable and she covers herself with enormous spiky rings and necklaces, and makes herself up like an idol. It amuses me to scare people, she says in her slow baritone, which bursts out like thunder in its sudden force. Powerful, dangerous, crushing, murderous, is the Amazon. And the fear she instils is always the same fear; it is the fear of our infantile and primitive *ancestors*, fear of scarring.

Before our marriage I had never mentioned my scar. Perhaps this is because as long as I can remember at my mother's instigation I had learned how to make myself up so as to hide completely what looked like a bruise: a web of veins, of purple, bluish fibres; of discoloured flesh and skin, often hot and beating like a pulse over the birthmark I had tried to excise. It became my special mark, the spot he would seek in love-making. We were spooked to see, later, that our child had inherited this birthmark. A strawberry.

The rain had eased into a drizzle. At last I was close to my destination. The road was wider and curving upwards. No paddocks bordered it. No houses anywhere. Not so much as the barking of a dog suggested human inhabitation. The black bodies of trees formed a ragged wall on each side. I slowed down, wary of kangaroos bounding across the road. Overhead, as I looked up between the windscreen wipers, shone a faint Southern Cross in the indigo sky. I scrutinised the wall of trees for the opening I knew was there, and veered right. I parked the car under a huge stringy bark. My heart started racing, and I had a bizarre sensation that was rather like being in love.

A dark purple night, an icy wind. The drizzling had stopped. Wind pounds and gets right inside you, unlike rain which pounds and skittles off. There was no track or any indication of a trail. I stomped my way through a thick outcropping of bushes and grass, driving my feet into the cracked ground, trampling dried twigs that exploded in showers of splinters despite the recent rain. I could hear the footloose creek at the base of the hill trickling on at its own pace under a canopy of scrub and creepers I remembered growing out of control.

There was something uncanny about the place, yet soothing. I called for a verb with some mysterious weight to bring back to life a dream's blank faces I willed with lidded eyes and fully fleshed lips. But words at that moment beat a retreat.

In my mind I painted the shadows. Every part of life has them, and in art, perhaps more obviously than anywhere else; it is the shadows that make the light and the colours believable. Black and white are absolutes—either the total absorption of light as you leave the world, or the total reflection of the light as you return to a state of luminosity. And violet is the last colour in the rainbow, the ending of the known and the beginning of the unknown—which is why it was so suitable for me to arrive as dawn was about to break.

Cold and aching all over, I could hardly breathe. I followed the path. I pushed the gate open, buttoned up my coat and made my way through the imposing grave stones to the baby white crosses at the back of the paddock. Here, in the violet light, I read the confirmation of my loss.

I went into the grave itself. Entered it. Sank into the inner dark. Sank further.

I have come to a boundary and feel the pressure exerted at that point where every membrane of existence is stretched taught like a drum between inner and outer worlds. At this point, in the sudden inversion of point and periphery, the spirits speak and are heard. As if hearing is responding and touch looses itself. As if the grave is dust.

Lipped lobelias

    break into song

        through the mist

The child has picked lemons from our backyard that smell so sweet and rhyme with storms. He is the king of the universe and because of him clouds darken and when you look out the window the world is a painted canvas.

Drop by drop, the sky, full of gossamer and grey, pours its heart out. Millions of baubles sparkle and dazzle. With each pelting, clouds seem to vanish and you can nearly hear a rainbow whooshing up from the earth's *omphalos*. The flame tree in the back garden is afire. A downpour of gold.

After the rain, a murder of crows, blue and green and gold as oil and as violet swoop on the tree where the child speaks to angels and ghosts. The whole house sways and it seems to rain again except that it's raining light. Leaves rustle and make a loud crackling on the roof. The day is stitched with points of light and all the threads make the lining of our world.

The child sits against the light at the table opposite me. He draws triangles in bright yellow. Looks up. His eyes are deep blue and glowing. He is not sad, but I can tell he is angry, for his pupils are smaller and look accusing. His brother's life; his brother's death, has made us strangers to each other.

> Mummy, how do stars die?
> Stars die when they've used up all their fuel, love.

The child gathers himself back into rhythm and resumes drawing. He draws a set of traffic lights. The amber circle is the largest one. He draws a boy with long saffron spidery limbs and hands with six fingers. He draws a purple sky full of pale yellow stars.

He draws and I write.

Soon, he will fidget on his chair. Soon, he will want to go for a walk. Soon, he will run amuck and wreck the cardboard boxes we save for making a *humongous* cubby-house.

The child does not know how to return to his place in his own life.

Outside the window, two kookaburras are circling together. One bird veers away, the other not seeming to notice. The first, larger bird returns to join the other's attentiveness. They fly on falling into distance until they break across a clump of she-oaks.

It is as though the child's imagination always stops short of some revelation.

It is as though he is lost in his thoughts just as you dream or suddenly drift off in thought. And he draws.

> Mummy, what will happen to the universe when the sun dies?
> I don't know, love. That would be catastrophic.
> What does *cataftrofic* mean?
> Terrible, I guess.

As the child draws, the mother, formerly myself, writes, for it makes sense. It coheres. It can be read.

There are signs in the Australian sky I cannot decipher. As a child, the vast and tangled ant-nest of triangles drawn through points of light in the northern hemisphere held the language of god. Never was I more enthralled than when I raised my eyes to the night's milk-stained dark purple and imagined a gold smattered blue atlas more awe-inspiring than the one Columbus owned—with its ocean the earth seemed to navigate. Now I know there are days great shipwrecks come with fear while we stretch out our necks as does old mother goose in our favourite book.

The child fidgets on his chair. The mother suggests a walk, but he doesn't *want* to.

Reluctantly, I gather myself, get up and make my way to the laundry. I fill a discarded ice-cream container with cold water, reach for the packet of Lux, pour a handful of soap flakes in the container and whisk them up in the water until they dissolve and thicken.

When I return to the living room, a mere extension of the kitchen, the child is furiously sketching a tree whose branches are a bunch of thick straight spikes opening up from a gnarly trunk. It looks like a deep brownish-red woodcut and I want yet don't want to touch it.

> Looks dangerous.
> Leave it alone. It *is* dangerous.
>
> Okay. What is it?
> A *dra*-gon's *blood* tree.

Now I see, but do not comment. I am so impressed. Dragon's blood tree, so called because its resin is so dark that it must be reptilian and therefore perilous. How the imagination crosses cultures and centuries. And I feel silly because I didn't listen properly to the story of safflower whose coloured resin is still highly prized for violins today as the child's father said last night.

> *Strangers to each other. A comedy of errors.*

Mummy, one more picture and we can go for a walk. I need to.

Great. I'll fix us some lunch. Honey sandwich?

No. An egg to dip in. And we need to buy lolly fruit. Apricots. Oranges, too, real ones because dad likes them and it's winter. We could also make a vitamin C cake.

Yes, child I will prove that I love you out of my cheer impotence, the mother does not say, but writes. *Food as love's metonymy. The more complex the task of cooking the better. Not that boiling an egg is a complex task, though it is when you are breast-feeding a little rival—little rascual, as you say.*

Yes. An egg to dip in sounds great. With sand bread fishes.
I like soldiers better.
All right love, let's soldier on.

I get up and I feed our cheap stereo system Mozart's symphony in F major, wash my hands, fetch a small pot from the drying rack, fill it with water and plunge three small eggs in—one for the child and two that I will boil hard for tomorrow's asparagus *à la flamande*. As I work I cannot help but watch the child, trying to inhabit his head, dreading it.

Writing is like walking, a single step dissolves what sticks into motion. The eye here and there rests on a leaf, gap, sign. Writing and walking as ways of connecting; of finding out the life of whatever it is one might accompany, either present or absent. Through constancy in change, through form and movement, the connective tissue of liveliness.

But what of drawing? Why does it stop short? Or am I asking the wrong question?

The dimension of writing—which has to do with the real and with time, separates itself from language. But so does drawing. You symbolise time. Subjectivise it—if such a verb exists.

Still, when the child walks it is as though he starts where his drawing left off. And when he sticks his hands in the whipped up Lux, the anger leaves him.

So, what is it? The world has been given to us and it is here, not new, though renewing, growing and decaying. Also greatly dying; and we are in it, longing for freshness, for the new, and anxiously impelled by Orpheus to see it anew.

The navel of the world.

Omphalos. Omphalos. Omphalos...

I glance at the new picture: a red house with no door, no windows.

Why is your house red?

Because the music is red, you silly, the child says pointing to the speakers that flank our ormolu clock.

The child's egg is ready. I scoop it up and flick it in his Humpty Dumpty eggcup. I slice off the crown and butter the sourdough, cut up the soldiers and serve him.

Voilà, mon roi.

Speak English.

I rest my hands on the table. He dips his buttery soldiers one by one into the soft orange yolk. When the eggshell is empty he plunges the spoon through to the bottom of the eggcup so that no witches can get hold of it and use it for a boat. He passes on the crown to me and I eat it.

Let's go!

We rug up and burst out the front door.

The child is running away from me, hair spiked up like a field of wheat in the moody August afternoon. It is surprisingly windy and chilly. I catch his right hand, reminding him of the safe side of the road, though conscious I am not too sure whose safety I am talking about. At the end of our street, we veer left. It is almost instinctual.

Though you don't believe in god, or at least say so, you are not surprised when the child climbs the steps to St Clements.

    Mummy, are clouds made of snow?

By the lonely steep climb towards the summit where the angels dwell to feed on nothing but honeyed snow...

The child's hand leads you straight to the sacrament chapel, the part of the church where the sacrament is reserved and where the physical becomes sublime and the sublime becomes physical.

Around the sacrament chapel is a carved procession of three violins and several lutes marching up the bare columns. In the choir stalls curving around the back of the altar you are drawn to some glowing spectacle.

You slip under the rope and see that behind each choir stall is a different picture made of the delicately varnished maple woods, spruce, cherry and walnut. A few scenes only are biblical. Most are secular. The distinctive one is the image of a lute, alone, on some mythical plane, waiting to be played.

Your breath is wasted on the air.

And then you realise the child is tugging at your hand.

When we get out the world has a new internal juncture. The child runs ahead on the disabled ramp. I cup my hands around my eyes against the glare and I shiver. I walk down the steps of the square and into the universe the king my child makes; and in the walking, an inner world is returned to me.

I feel myself accompanied. It is an intimate acquaintance.

Absent. And death is present in the pupils of the absent eyes, the holes in the mask that summons them, not us: he who advances masked and she who advances veiled.

Emptied of images I turn porous to absence. Become vast with absence. Then there is this holding breath in the gasp of surprise. The child has broken into song.

> *Gay go up and Gay go down,*
> *To ring the bells of London Town.*
>
> *Bull's eyes and targets...*

The child is about to run across the road.

The mother grips her son's hand. Firmly.

Tomorrow we'll buy modelling clay.

What's modelling clay?

It's like *play-dad*.

Okay. Tonight then, let's not sing *Twinkle Twinkle Little Star*.

Broken toys

    litter the street

        Baudelaire where are you?

Languid, I lol about in a listless garden, reading again about being pregnant. The snail creeper on our fence is all entangled and full of heady scent. The ants love it. Swarm about deep inside the flowers. Untouched, a box of pastels lies next to the notebook at my feet. My ankles swell with the heat. I feel dizzy and slightly nauseous. The brash sunlight makes me irritable. I long for cooler days, splashes of swallows and grass parrots.

This is the child every woman wants. The child women who don't want children pine for despite themselves; the child women who abort want restored; the child women who can't have them desire so strongly; the child women who plan ahead design. The child there, not there. The child who comes and goes like the reel. *Fort. Da!*

> In the flesh of your dreams.

> The child alive.

> A quickening of meaning.

You list and discard dangers: wild beasts, prowlers, storms at sea.

Tongue of the world archiving loss in the communal vault.

A sentence rises up, hovers in the air, drifts...

expecting is about encounters with that which is both within and without, real and imaginary, present and future extending their magnetic attraction on the axis of the past

> OR expecting takes you out and outside of yourself

> OR expecting takes you through it and to extremes

> **OOOOOOOOOR...**

> *expecting is about encounters*
> *both within and without,*
> *real and imaginary.*
>
> *Present and future extending*
> *their magnetic attraction on the axis of the past.*
>
> *OR*
> *expecting takes you*
> *out and outside of yourself*
>
> *OR*
> *expecting takes you*
> *through it and to extremes*

A smudging of green-blue takes shape against white, indigo, aquamarine.

You are a *corsaire, a corps-serre* / a corsair, a body greenhouse & body holding tight.

    Word, colour, dream incarnate.

    Word, colour, dream extimate.

Tense and worried, I muck about in a crowded garden, thinking again about being pregnant. The snail creeper on our fence is all entangled and full of heady seed. The ants love it. Swarm about from deep inside the flowers. Barely touched, a box of pastels lies next to the notebook on the bench. My ankles sweat inside my boots. I feel scatty and slightly nauseous. The grey light makes me irritable. I long for warmer days, splashes of honey-eaters and kookaburras.

This is the child every woman wants. The child women who don't want children pine for despite themselves; the child women who abort want restored; the child women who can't have them desire so strongly; the child women who plan ahead design. The child not there already there. The child who goes and comes like the reel. *Fort. Da!*

    In the aliveness of your dreams, the child made flesh.

    A meaning for quickening.

You list and discard dangers: wild beasts, prowlers, storms at sea.

Tongue of the world archiving loss in the communal vault.

A sentence rears up, hovers in the air, drifts...

expecting is about encounters with that which is both within and without, real and imaginary, past and future extending their magnetic attraction on the axis of the present

    OR expecting takes you in and outside of yourself

    OR expecting takes you through onto extremes

A smudging of blue-green takes shape from white, indigo, aquamarine.

You are a *corsaire, a serre-corps* / a corsair, a body holding tight, a body greenhouse...*corpuscule étiolé dans le rêve* éveillé / spangled corpuscle in a waking dream.

    Dream, colour, word incarnate.

    Dream, colour, word extimate.

Languid and lazy, I lol about in a listless garden.

This is the child every woman wants.

In the flesh of your dreams, the child alive.

A quickening of meaning.

A sentence rises up, hovers in the air, drifts...

Double sun

    hope lies

        better than a smirking child

Sunday. Still and grey. Not a breath of wind. Love-in-the-mist is struggling through. Snow drops are in bloom. The sky is an ashen blue in between blankets of grey clouds. A bird I know nothing of cries out again as it did at night, keeping me awake. An uncanny, disturbing cry as if the bird itself were being choked again and again.

Frost. I had dreamed of putting in seeds again today. Poppies. Raking the soil to make it fine and even. Scattering the seeds over, raking, watering, marking the spot with a stick. Watering again. Trying a different method since I have trouble growing seeds where they are to grow. It's a shame. I think I bury them too deeply.

Silence. The rustle of my own breathing.

I am a coffin cold as stone.

In the shower the water whistles and makes a loud crackling sound. I burst into tears. My body heaves and shakes. Heaves and shakes. Heaves and shakes the inconsolable sorrow that inhabits me and seems to grow and grow from nowhere and pushes into my heart, bones, flesh.

Against the heavy sky lives a woman who repeats *mes mots* / my words with her sob sobbing and at times like these I don't know why I hold her close. Like shadows coffined in broad daylight.

And then I remember. It is thirteen years since we buried the newly born, the one whose name can no longer be spoken, the one whose name in my fictions begins with U.

> *Human beings are like rivers; the water is one and the same in all of them.*

Black birds gather like a frown. A studied frown this time around. The clouds thicken into ridges, pressing the ashen blue into the grey. Pressing the passing of time. Not at all the way you would expect, but the body remembers.

U. The letter. The name of the baby in utero when we didn't know. Didn't know. Didn't know.

U. So dependent and yet so folded-in to itself—so separate—of itself.

A letter made for each newly born, so folded-in to itself—so separate.

Despite the transformations of pronouns.

And all too soon and too suddenly: a doll's face. Wax face. Small and smooth and shiny. White dappled with purple that is darkened on one side of the nose by a wash of blood.

Black moss

Stone flesh

    Cradle grave

Nothing reflects back

Soon the brothers will barge in and break the unbroken tie that curves inside.

I compose myself

put U on the long finger

No time for waffles. I could make a cake, but that would be suspicious. I decide on bread and butter pudding. Some sunshine in all this blackness.

Putting on my clothes, a feeling of sadness washes over me like white sunlight that slides down a wall as though love in my heart has grown cold.

I scurry down the stairs past the soft toys cupboard, getting lost in my thoughts.

What I'll need is to preheat the oven (190 C) and stick to the recipe, which I rarely do.

> A handful of sultanas
> 2 large slices of white bread—crusts that I remove, and butter
> a pinch of nutmeg
> 3 eggs beaten with energy
> five spoons of caster sugar
> a lime of which I grate ½ teaspoon, taking care of fingernails
> 250 ml cream—and mix

I butter an oven-proof dish and sprinkle half the sultanas over the bottom; layer the bread butter-side up in the dish; whisk the eggs, sugar, lime and cream together; sprinkle the remaining sultanas with a cloud of nutmeg on top and put it in the oven. It will have to bake for 45 minutes. Meanwhile I check there is Greek yoghurt to serve with. Yes!

Plates are laid on the table. Forks and spoons. A late camellia blossom in a saucer. Time will finish off the work.

A car door slams shut.

Hurried footsteps on the concrete stairs, and the door bursts open.

> Mum, we are off to watch the world cup this afternoon, says the first-born with three approving brothers and their father in tow.

It is almost in astonishment that I realise life goes on, after all, and marvel at the first-born's will to live and experience new things. I am in awe of this will to overcome the terror that must have been awakened in him by the certainty of his own death, thirteen years ago, a knowledge that he could possibly neither know nor comprehend, a knowledge of something that was and is outside time and outside the world as we know it.

Death. This absolute. The ineffable that eludes presence and yet makes the other, the loved one, even more present than things in actual life will ever do. With a presence so insistent that when we are not learning how to tame it we occupy ourselves trying to find a way of escaping its clutches in writing. It is this strange presence of death, liable to occur at any moment, that makes it the unwelcome guest at our table with its bread and pudding meant to celebrate life.

Death as that singular fear of finitude against a background of black light.

They eat. They eat with consideration. Or perhaps this is my own interpretation.

> *Mourning is a smudging*
>
> *the stream so thin now*
> *that it must be near—the source,*
> *as far from the surface world.*

Mourning is the experience of death in remembering, in being with the dead; it is a sublation of death and a strategy destined to fill the caesura made by grief, the discontinuity of temporality in which death means being hostage to a ghost. And beyond, in cloudless skies, that ghost and a trail of them reach back. To say *deceased* is a flight from the brutal reality of loss: death as a natural accident that happens everyday, perhaps only to others. There is a distancing from death itself, and from the dimension of mourning that entails the resolution of the psychical conflict imbedded in the etymological proximity of *deuil* and *duel* in the Old French. *Eros* and *Thanatos* crossing swords, so to speak. The old battle ever newly restaged. Restaging a primal loss.

I do it now. With this writing and so wonder whether this is solution or ritual. Or both. Whether it is normal or pathological. Whether there is a difference between mourning and melancholia as Freud thought in 1914 before his daughter died.

> Mournfully tending toward what has been lost. Tending it. And for no clear purpose.
>
> Troping into night and death to keep love alive.
>
> Writing the thing itself, magma, lava, *boue noire* / black mud liquefying ash. Shh. Shh. Shh.

Perhaps writing, especially poetry, is the art of loss. It is the blanks that are pressing. And what I hear through the interstices of words presses back to a kind of writing translated from the dark. It's like encrypting an enigma. For one moment I am in this interval between two modes of expression, and often, two languages, neither in one or the other, poised on the brink of some petrified mass of aesthetic conventions as well as tongues. It's an unsettling process. Exhilarating. Terrifying. It all depends on how the echoes spread in the crypt. Making silence or music.

Writing as perpetual *Fort. Da!* Reinscribing bits and pieces, *des restes*, remnants and revenants *dans des récits* that shift back and forth back and forth from one medium to another, mode to another, tongue to another, thing to another. *Rengaines*.

Going back to a (non)origin. The birth and death of meaning.

Une mise en abîme to write of desire, of water and fire.

Writing
undoing difference
inking difference
the difference within
the difference without

Inkingthedifferencewithinthedifferencewithout

writing from it

away from it

The mark of infidel fidelity

FIDELITY, from the French *fidélité* or the Latin *fidelitas*; see FEALTY, which means the obligation of fidelity. XIV ME *feau(l)te, fealte* (mod. *féauté*): L. *fidelitas*, at, f. *fidelis* faithful, f. *fides* FAITH

    because *every soul is a rhythmic knot*, said Mallarmé

    because I hear FAULT in *feau(l)te* and because I am matter
    mater

    le corps lieu d'attache ultime de la parole et de ses effets matériels et aussi le chantoir—source productive multiple des conditions du sens et du non-sens

    the body ultimate anchoring point of speech and of its material effects and also the wellspring—manifold creative source of the conditions of sense and non-sense

    and as such know I can give life and death

      [a knot is a stone is a screen is a shroud unravelling]

D.H.

un coup de dé / a dice throw

une ex-halaison / a last breath

une hache / an axe & the sharp cut

the heitch été agapé and the gap in love

[a knot is a stone is a screen is a shroud unravelling]

[life and death *in-bedded* in me. Ambivalently nurturing and violent]

life and death déchaînées / unleashing & unlinked

There is a Persian myth of the creation of the world. In that myth a woman creates the world, and she does so through the power of her own sex, which, of course cannot be duplicated by men. It is *natural*; it is *awesome*. And she gives birth to a great number of sons. The sons, seriously puzzled, become frightened. What is this creative urge? This creative act? And why can't they duplicate it? Who can tell us, they ask, if she can give life, she can also take it away? And so, because of this enigmatic ability of woman, including all reversible possibilities, they kill her.

Loss is one with deliverance and the death of meaning.

From text to text in a movement of endless deliverance I cannot free myself of you, and that is fidelity.

Liebestod.

Lorikeets cackle

in the pear tree

góreckiorff

We now live in our own house at the edge of the city: a luminous structure jutting out of a hill above the Merri Creek, with both sunlight and moonlight reflecting on stainless steel surfaces. It is a changeable house, too. It stands its ground solidly deflecting the heat of the sun, but it rocks like a boat in the wind, winter, spring, summer, fall. What binds this house is the sky. From my fiction room I can see the city skyline slowly emerging from the night as lights are flicked on in offices. It is a house with its own integrity of life lived, dreamed and made.

It is now time to finish the book in which I sought the face of a child, the voice of some twin, the book in which I found the face of the moon and a disconcerting multiplicity of voices stirring the shadows all about—rumours that prised me from myself only to fade, restoring me to some clamour only to leave me dispossessed. With nothing on my hands but time. With time, yes, life went on. With time life went on as I watched my first-born learning to organise it into *now, yesterday, tomorrow*. With time we made other children and our children made things. And I made the music I could no longer bear to listen to.

    Why is white white?

    Chalk, rice, zinc
        Crystal falls
            Limestone graves

    Phosphorus
        Lightless body
            Alabaster

Fifteen years of life lived at dream's edge. Fifteen years of hands meeting needs to *posséder la* vérité dans une âme *et un corps* / to take possession of truth within a single soul and body, as Rimbaud said. Fifteen years of writing limits, looking for latent truths, finding buried knowledge. And the ultimate truth in between grief and guilt.

All this at the expense of losing your mother tongue and cracking your own voice. But I, myself, kept alive as I turned affect into feeling, feeling into emotion, memories into fiction, fiction into being in a relentless process of littering and lettering loss, hope, love.

It is a matter of existing within that polarity—between the white centre and the vast periphery, between the black in the white and the colours in the light.

>To exist is to stitch a wound.

>To write is nothing but to stitch a wound with a child's hand.

>Hand Star of David
>*vide-la*
>*tu la vis*
>*la vida*
>words emptying out

>Vacant in the silence within

>Stitch ouch itch *we eee*

>I am doing it again

>fragmenting my narrative as I feel the anxiety rising

>cutting up sentences / words / reaching for the letter / through metaphor *eee*

>I cut the lethal umbilical cord that binds me to Time.

>*Mountain strawberries are hardy plants*
>   *... I wipe the red off my hands*

The dynamic involving grief and narcissistic delusion comes to a head in the image of the hand. The hand becomes a star and so stops meaning in its tracks. Though the star names the dead child, it firmly inscribes him in culture, albeit with the heavy legacy it bears in the Judeo-Christian tradition. David is now outside of me. Memorialised. Through mourning, a mourning that entails fragments and a passage from prose to poetry, from sense to non-sense, *sang rouge* to *sang blanc*.

The fragment as the embodiment of the energy needed to begin. A beginning that involves reinventing the notion of endings, of death and loss. And so from prose to poetry, because metaphor touches towards the unsaid unsayable in the new beginning while metonymy only says what can be said.

And so from the black of my heart I trick myself to write out the white into glitter.

To untie myself from the world. To tie myself to it. In *Engelish* (says my last-born).

In the volcano's eye at Lake Taupo in New Zealand where generations of granite lay mute under water and stones float on water I watched my children tumble and splash as I grappled with fire words for the incandescent ending to their brother's book. In the volcano's eye all was slipstream of light, pumice and gleaming water. All aglitter. And on the surface of the water where cold volcanic ash shimmered a child's face drifted across. On the shore froze a salamander in mid flight.

> I am a salamander
>
> crawling through fire
>
> caught in your gaze
>
> *un* / harmed

Would you say poetic discourse can transmute the spectre of death and regenerate desire? Would you say, when poetry collapses, death unwinds the textures which bind us to desire itself?

At Lake Taupo at the end of the earth I was out of time. I was inside Time. I saw in the mirrored reflection on the surface of the water in the crater formed by the volcano what Narcissus saw and what Orpheus looked for. Ghosts are *go-betweens*. They tell us where death resides. Where life is. They tell us that art is an entwining of death and life and what lies *in-between*. They tell us that *one writes because one has to create a world in which one can live*. At the end of the earth I came full-circle. *Shh.*

Letter by letter, on the litter of another language I have stopped the torrent of grief and *jouissance* that would have been the end of me had I written in my mother tongue. Mother. *Mater.* Matter.

In another language I am matter's light. Shadow's light. The future, not the past.

'T is done. I have put death to death. I have returned the night to the night. For now.

Smell the intoxicating scent of jasmine—the way it clings. The life and death of scent, the absence clinging, rustling, like a voice.

    Eurydice, Eurydice, Eurydice.

From the window of my fiction room I can see the light now slanting through the trees, mottling the garden with golden speckles, overshadowing daybreak's smatter of crumpled shadows. Steam rises from the ground as if the earth itself is being boiled from inside out. The day is fresh, streaming with flecks of light and dust. All is pure rhythm. All pulsating glitter. A pre-inscription.

There are splashes of silver everywhere in a grey green, grey blue landscape. A flush of oxidized copper green spreads in the Japanese cherry by the front stairs. Spring is here in a hurry. Two rainbow lorikeets swoop into the camphor laurel next to the window to eat the berries. The sap running on the bark of the blackwood looks like honey. Honey-spangle day.

Even from this window the Australian sky is huge, the middle distance hazily expansive. A sky to get lost in, float, find a soul exfoliating itself.

Sunlight sparkles and crystallises in the breeze that comes from Bass Straight.

I am becoming other, but nothing like the expected antipodean transplant you would have expected. I am an extimate exile.

As the din of dawn dies I listen to the nothing there—this still inarticulate speech of the heart. And I want to tell them about the shrieks and colours of the lorikeets. I want to tell them about the sky. I want to tell them how their sky is now my alphabet. I want to tell them about the gratitude I feel for the weird conjunction of events that brought me here where in the budding branches of the bushes and trees and in the light I see sky words. In these sky words is light's eye, the source of metaphors, a curious and persistent feature of the natural world that language leads us into: a minute attention to spottiness in things, an attention so marked that we sometimes have the impression of an obsessively pointillist word painter at work behind the scene. This word painter I call the spirit child.

References

In the wings you will hear whispers by Antonin Artaud, Yves Bonnefoy, Jorge Luis Borges, Maurice Carême, Lewis Carroll, Hélène Cixous, Gilles Deleuze, Marguerite Duras, Paul Éluard, Janet Frame, Julia Kristeva, Martin Heidegger, Philip Hodgins, Luce Irigaray, Francis Jammes, James Joyce, Jacques Prévert, Raymond Queneau, Sidney Wade, Ngugi Wa Thiongo and many others who have sustained my love of words. The following works inform the work obliquely or are quoted from, as per page numbers:

Barthes, R. (1953) *Le Degré zéro de l'écriture*. Paris: Seuil.

Barthes, R. (1975) *Roland Barthes*. Paris: Seuil.

Barthes, R. (1977 [1973]) 'The Grain of the Voice' *Image, Music, Text*. tr. Stephen Heath. London: Fontana, pp. 79-89.

Derrida, J. (1974) *Glas*. Paris: Denoël.

Eluard, P. (1972) *Capitale de la douleur, suivi de L'Amour de la poésie*. Paris: Gallimard, p. 191.

Farmer, B. (1990) *A Body of Water*. St Lucia: University of Queensland Press.

Finlay, V. (2002) *Colour*. London: Sceptre.

Freud, S. (2001 [1914-1916]) 'Mourning and melancholia' *The Standard Edition of the Complete Psychological Works of Sigmund Freud, Vol. XIV: On the History of the Psycho-Analytic Movement, Papers on Metapsychology and Other Works*, James Strachey, ed. London: Vintage, The Hogarth Press and the Institute of Psycho-analysis.

Freud, S. (2001 [1920-1922]) *The Standard Edition of the Complete Psychological Works of Sigmund Freud, Vol. XVIII: Beyond the Pleasure Principle, Group Psychology and Other Works*, James Strachey, ed. London: Vintage, The Hogarth Press and the Institute of Psycho-analysis.

Grigg, R. (2015) 'Melancholia and the unabandoned object' in Patricia Gherovici & Manya Steinkoler, eds. *Lacan on Madness*. London & New York: Routledge, pp. 139-59.

Gross, P. (2013) *Caves of Making*. Newmarket: The Professional and Higher Partnership, p. 9.

Heaney, S. (1966) *Death of a Naturalist*. London: Faber, p. 13.

Heaney, S. (1980) *Preoccupations: Selected Prose, 1968-1978*. London: Faber & Faber, p. 46.

Lacan, J. (1998 [1972-73]) *Encore: on Feminine sexuality, the Limits of Love and Knowledge, tr. Bruce Fink*. New York: Norton.

Lacan, J. (2001 [1971]) 'Lituraterre', in Jacques Lacan, Jacques-Alain Miller, ed. *Autres Ecrits*. Paris: Seuil.

Lacan, J. (2005 [1975-76]) *Le Séminaire, livre XXIII. Le sinthome,* Jacques-Alain Miller, ed. Paris: Seuil.

Lacan, J. (1994 [1956-57]) *Le Séminaire, livre IV. La relation d'objet,* Jacques-Alain Miller, ed. Paris: Seuil.

Lacan, J. (2006) *Ecrits, tr. Bruce Fink* New York: Norton.

Lacan, J. (2006 [1971-72]) *Le* séminaire, livre XVIII. D'un discours qui ne serait pas du semblant, Jacques-Alain Miller, ed. Paris: Seuil.

Mallarmé, S. (1973) 'Le Mystère dans les lettres' *Oeuvres Complètes* Paris: Gallimard, p. 387.

Nin, A. (1992) *In Favour of the Sensitive Man and Other Essays*. Harmondsworth: Penguin, p. 12.

Rimbaud, A. (1966) Complete Works, Selected Letters, William Fowlie, ed. Chicago: University of Chicago Press, p. 208.